Sobriety For Christmas

Gregory Madison

AWE OF MY LIFE PUBLICATIONS
AWE IN AWE

Sobriety for Christmas

AWE OF MY LIFE PUBLICATIONS
www.turningtoGodfromidols.com

Cover photo by Vince_Lamb

ISBN- 978-0-9701209-1-5

Contents

Introduction

Just like our Christmas presents addictions come in all different shapes and sizes. And while we tend to focus on the shopaholics idolatry during the Advent, the Christmas message is big enough to address the opioid crisis, pornographic craze, alcoholism and every other addiction that would draw our highest attention.

The highest form of sobriety known to mankind is in Jesus Christ. The Christmas story is filled with sobriety in that it draws conviction. Conviction is defined as **a settled persuasion**, the state of being **convinced**. It is the story of how God is so much greater than we could ever imagine. Greater than the idols we would construct. In this story, we are told that God wants to be personally involved with each and every one of us. For this reason, the Christmas story, also, contains serenity (a major component of sobriety) marked by contentment.

But we see turbulence and confusion within the Christmas story, as well. These are some of the traits of our addictions (better known as idols). One of the definitions for an idol comes from the New Unger's Bible Dictionary. **An idol is "an empty thing, rendered elsewhere 'trouble,' 'iniquity,' 'vanity,' 'wickedness,' etc.**

The Christmas story is incomplete without the significance of its main character!

The Incomparable Christ

More than nineteen hundred years ago, there was a Man born contrary to the laws of life. This Man lived in poverty and was reared in obscurity. He did not travel extensively. Only once did He cross the boundary of the country in which He lived; that was during His exile in childhood.

He possessed neither wealth nor influence. His relatives were inconspicuous and had neither training nor formal education.

In infancy He startled a king; in childhood He puzzled doctors; in manhood He ruled the course of nature, walked upon the waves as pavement, and hushed the sea to sleep.

He healed the multitudes without medicine and made no charge for His service.

He never wrote a book, and yet perhaps all the libraries of the world could not hold the books that have been written about Him.

He never wrote a song, and yet He has furnished the theme for more songs than all the songwriters combined.

He never founded a college, but all the schools put together cannot boast of having as many students.

He never marshaled an army, nor drafted a soldier, nor fired a gun; and yet no leader ever had more volunteers who have, under His orders, made more rebels stack arms and surrender without a shot fired.

He never practiced psychiatry, and yet He has healed more broken hearts than all the doctors far and near.

Once each week multitudes congregate at worshiping assemblies to pay homage and respect to Him.

The names of the past, proud statesmen of Greece and Rome have come and gone. The names of the past scientists, philosophers, and theologians have come and gone. But the name of this Man multiplies more and more. Though time has spread nineteen hundred years between the people of this generation and the mockers at His crucifixion, He still lives. His enemies could not destroy Him, and the grave could not hold Him.

He stands forth upon the highest pinnacle of heavenly glory, proclaimed of God, acknowledged by angels, adored by saints, and feared by devils, as the risen, personal Christ, our Lord and Savior.

And while the Christmas story is not complete without its main character, the Christmas story will not do without you either! ALL OF YOU!

Room for Jesus

And she brought forth her firstborn son, and wrapped him in swaddling clothes, and laid him in a manger; because there was no room for them in the inn.
Luke 2:7

I have been blessed with the opportunity to participate in a program called "The Room in the Inn" where churches across the state of Tennessee are asked to welcome the homeless to lodge at their church during the months of November through March. The whole idea is that while there was no room for Jesus on the day that He was born, there is room for the homeless at these churches.

And not only that, there is room at the cross for everyone (as the old folks used to say). The question is often asked of whether you have room for Jesus. Addictions can take up so much space that there is no room for anything else. If we make room for Jesus, we will have the truth that is in Jesus and be filled with the truth. On the contrary, the more room that we give to addictions, the more falsehood and confusion there is.

I love the way that some equate our lives to a house and that being filled with the Spirit means that when we allow God access into every area of our lives it is like welcoming Him into every room of our house, I, also, like a piece of writing by C.S. Lewis.

"I think that many of us, when Christ has enabled us to overcome one or two sins that were an obvious nuisance, are inclined to feel (though we do not put it into words) that we are now good enough. He has done all we wanted Him to do, and we should be obliged if he would leave us alone. But the question is not what we intended ourselves to be, but what he intended us to be when he made us…imagine yourself as a living house. God comes in to rebuild that house. At first. Perhaps, you can understand what he is doing. He is getting the drains right and stopping the leaks in the roof and so on. You knew that those jobs needed doing and so you are not surprised. But presently he starts knocking the house about in a way that hurts abominably and does not seem to make sense. What on earth is he up to? The explanation is that he is building quite a different house from the one you thought of-throwing out a new wing here, putting on an extra floor there, running up towers, making courtyards. You thought you were going to be made into a decent little cottage, but he is building a palace. He intends to come and live in it himself."

Counsel

For to us a child is born, to us a son is given, and the government will be on his shoulders. And he will be called Wonderful Counselor, Mighty God, Everlasting Father, Prince of Peace.
Isaiah 9:6

No one in their right mind would deny that those who are subject to succumb to addictions need counsel. The question is- where is that counsel coming from?

Again, and again I say that **the highest form of sobriety is found in Christ**. Just as there is no greater love that a man has than to lay down his life, as Jesus did, there is no greater counsel than from Jesus (that's because His counsel is based on His love).

One of the resources that God used to initiate my sobriety is a book called "All the Messianic Prophecies of the Bible" by Herbert Lockyer. It is quite sobering to discover that everything that was said of Jesus long before His first advent has come to past. Lockyer states that, "According to the law of compound probabilities, the chance that they all happened together by accident is 1 in 537,000,000."

Jesus gave a lot of counsel during His first advent. Just one example is where He was yet a child and He astonished the learned of His day (Luke 2:46-47). I can, personally, say that Jesus has counseled and continues to counsel on an individual basis those who seek Him. And then we come to the counsel that He gives prior to His second advent, which is **highly applicable to those of us who are subject to succumb to addictions**.

I counsel you to buy from me gold refined in the fire, so you can become rich; and white clothes to wear, so you can cover your shameful nakedness; and salve to put on your eyes, so you can see. Revelation 3:18

Your Significance

"But you, Bethlehem Ephrathah, though you are small among the clans of Judah, out of you will come for me one who will be ruler over Israel, whose origins are from of old, from ancient times." Micah 5:2

Addictions can make us feel small, insignificant, useless, even worthless. But, just as Jesus made Bethlehem significant, useful and of value, He does the same for us!

Trouble

Now when Jesus was born in Bethlehem of Judaea in the days of Herod the king, behold, there came wise men from the east to Jerusalem, Saying, Where is he that is born King of the Jews? for we have seen his star in the east, and are come to worship him. When Herod the king had heard these things, he was troubled, and all Jerusalem with him. Matthew 2:3

I'm overwhelmingly grateful that God began to show me the connection between addictions and idolatry as far back as 1995. Somewhere in my studies, I decided to find out the deeper meaning of idolatry by reading the definition for the various Hebrews words that are used in the Bible translated in English as "idol". The definition of one of the words was "a troublesome thing". Surely, this is an adequate description of addictions as well. I shouldn't have to go into detail. If you have not discovered this for yourself, just ask someone!

Now, here's the question that confronts us whenever we are tempted to turn towards an addiction.

What's the trouble with Jesus? Is it that we, like Herod, have a problem with His Kingship?

One thing that I can almost say, beyond 'a shadow of a doubt' is that we are either troubled with Jesus' presence or we are joyful. But then, it is all a matter of choice.

Joy and Delight

And he sent them to Bethlehem, and said, Go and search diligently for the young child; and when ye have found him, bring me word again, that I may come and worship him also. When they had heard the king, they departed; and, lo, the star, which they saw in the east, went before them, till it came and stood over where the young child was. When they saw the star, they rejoiced with exceeding great joy. Matthew 2:8-10

Thrill and delight is something that we seek in addictions. Wise men find this and more in seeking Christ. Just look at what 1 Peter 1:6-8 says!

Wherein ye greatly rejoice, though now for a season, if need be, ye are in heaviness through manifold temptations: That the trial of your faith, being much more precious than of gold that perisheth, though it be tried with fire, might be found unto praise and honour and glory at the appearing of Jesus Christ: Whom having not seen, ye love; in whom, though now ye see him not, yet believing, ye rejoice with joy unspeakable and full of glory. (KJV)

We rejoice in that of which we find value.

Just think of the value that is placed on addictions! People give up their very lives over addictions! How refreshing it is to own up to the worth of Christ. I would rather strive to express the true value of Christ than to try and express the value of an idol (addictions) which has no worth. It is here that the first question of the Westminster Catechism has a deeper, clearer, richer, fuller significance.

Q. What is the chief end of man? A. Man's chief end is to glorify God, and to enjoy him forever.

Christ vs. Addiction

And the Word was made flesh, and dwelt among us, (and we beheld his glory, the glory as of the only begotten of the Father) full of grace and truth.
John 1:14

While Jesus Christ is full of grace and truth, addictions are full of disgrace and falsehood. But let's just take a closer look at grace and truth and see how it has the power to conquer addictions.

Grace

For ye know the grace of our Lord Jesus Christ, that, though he was rich, yet for your sakes he became poor, that ye through his poverty might be rich.
2 Corinthians 8:9 (KJV)

In Christ- riches
Addictions- poverty (spiritually, materially for many)

For the grace of God that bringeth salvation hath appeared to all men, Teaching us that, denying ungodliness and worldly lusts, we should live soberly, righteously, and godly, in this present world;
Titus 2:11-12 (KJV)

In Christ- vision, salvation, education, godliness, restraint, sobriety.
Addictions- blindness, ruin, ignorance, the bondage of lust (for whatever the addiction is)

Truth

Let not mercy and truth forsake thee: bind them about thy neck; write them upon the table of thine heart: So shalt thou find favour and good understanding in the sight of God and man.
Proverbs 3:3-4 (KJV)

In Christ- harmony and peace
Addictions- strife and confusion (turmoil)

Then said Jesus to those Jews which believed on him, If ye continue in my word, then are ye my disciples indeed; And ye shall know the truth, and the truth shall make you free.
John 8:31-32 (KJV)

In Christ- enlightenment, consistency, stability, freedom
Addiction- darkness, inconsistency, instability, bondage

Now this is but a glimpse of the grace and truth that is found in Christ Jesus compared to the disgrace and falsity of addiction. Just imagine if we were to expound even farther! I believe that it would eventually prove to be inexhaustible!

Offending God

And she shall bring forth a son, and thou shalt call his name Jesus: for he shall save his people from their sins.
Matthew 1:21

I'm afraid of the trend that has started (I cannot tell you when).

When people talk about sin, they often discuss the harm that it causes individuals rather than sin (first and foremost) being an offense to a loving and holy God.

And so, as we consider what is the wrong of addiction then it is best to start with how it affects God.

There is no other belief that offers forgiveness of sin in a real and tangible manner outside of faith in the blood of Christ (check for yourself!). Another thing that I love about looking to Jesus to deal with addiction is that He doesn't just stop just there. Jesus is concerned about all sin. I am so very grateful that He can recognize just 'where I need to be saved' (though I may think that I'm alright). This reminds me of the phrase "deceitfulness of sin (found in Hebrews). And so, **if Jesus is the truth (as He said and I believe) and sin is so deceitful (which it is), then Jesus can and does certainly save his people from their sins.**

Behold

Behold, a virgin shall be with child, and shall bring forth a son, and they shall call his name Emmanuel, which being interpreted is, God with us.
Matthew 1:23

"Behold" was the word that was emphasized in a recital for the Christmas concert at my church. It really got my interest because I once read and meditated on all the times that the word 'behold' is used in scripture. We see "behold" used at least 9 times in the Gospels pertaining to the birth of Christ. When someone beckons us to behold, they are saying that this is worthy of our attention.

We behold that which interests us. That which we behold causes us to stop and pause. Addictions are beheld by many.

I would 'drop everything' for the sake of my addictions. On the contrary, that which is of Christ is infinitely worthy of our interests, our attentions, and, yes, even our affections.

Confusion vs. Clarity

Therefore, the Lord himself shall give you a sign; Behold, a virgin shall conceive, and bear a son, and shall call his name Immanuel.
Isaiah 7:14

Nobody in their right mind likes to be in the state of confusion. And that is just what an addiction has to offer. In fact, one of the Hebrew words for "idol" is "a confusion" (of course we know that the spiritual definition of an addiction is idolatry). The prophecy of Christ is very clear (though it may be hard to believe). Contrary to what some may believe, God is not in the 'guessing game'. Addiction can make you wonder if God really loves you. Addictions can, also, lead you to doubt the presence of God. It is only in Christ that we are assured of God's love and His presence. This is the basis of our hope. And it is not something that is just 'made up' says Peter.

For we have not followed cunningly devised fables, when we made known unto you the power and coming of our Lord Jesus Christ, but were eyewitnesses of his majesty. We have also a more sure word of prophecy; Whereunto ye do well that ye take heed, as unto a light that shineth in a dark place, until the day dawn, and the day star arise in your hearts:
2 Peter 1:16,19

Of course, we know that "Immanuel" means God with us. The presence of the Lord always has and always will make a difference. Look at what Moses said:

And he said unto him, If thy presence go not with me, carry us not up hence.
Exodus 33:15 KJV

There are many, many other passages that we can site, but the point that I am making is that **the presence of God offers the stability and security that we cannot find anywhere else (especially not in an addiction)**!

The Return of Christ

And, behold, there was a man in Jerusalem, whose name was Simeon; and the same man was just and devout, waiting for the consolation of Israel: and the Holy Ghost was upon him. And it was revealed unto him by the Holy Ghost, that he should not see death, before he had seen the Lord's Christ. Luke 2:25-26

As with many of the verses that we explore, there are so very many things that we could mention concerning addiction in today's passage. What is initially amazing about this passage for me is the correlation between Simeon waiting for the first advent of Christ and our waiting for the second advent of Christ and how it relates to our abstinence from addictions. I am very grateful for Edward T. Welch, who discusses the importance of this principle in his book "Addictions: A Banquet in the Grave". Welch states that the benefits of meditating on the return of Christ in regards to addictions are:

1. It reminds us that there is a deadline. The battle with sin is hard, but it will someday be over.

2. Eternity reveals the things that are important. When we are preoccupied with the present, our less-than-attentive consciences are more likely to permit "one more". But when we consider our thoughts and actions in the light of the return of Christ, the self-serving nature of our desires becomes more apparent.
3. It reveals our true destiny.

He ends this section of writing by stating, "We were created for something much more noble than eating feces. We were created to have passions that are directed to the glory of God."

In addition, there are many verses that encourage us to keep in mind the return of Christ as we strive to live a godly life. For the sake of brevity, I will just list a few of these references.

Matt. 25:1-13
Rom. 13:11-14
1 Thes. 1:9-10
Titus 2:12-13
1 John 2:28

Defining Sobriety

And Simeon blessed them, and said unto Mary his mother, Behold, this child is set for the fall and rising again of many in Israel; and for a sign which shall be spoken against,
Luke 2:34

Perhaps, the soberest moment in all of history is the moment that God took on human flesh.

While sobriety is a term that is often used to describe abstinence from alcoholic beverages, it carries a deeper, broader meaning than people usually realize.

The word sobriety is derived from the word sober, which means to be abstemious or not intoxicated. It, also, carries the meaning of being serious, solemn, devoid of frivolity, excess, or exaggeration, marked by circumspection and self-restraint, temperate, exercising cool reason, and subdued. Other words for "sober" are: sedate, earnest, moderate, wise, sane, humility, senses, truth. The Biblical definitions relating to being sober have to do with being discreet, watchful, of sound mind or sane, and disciplined, having self-control.

And so, it is sobriety of mind that leads to sobriety from addiction. Sober thinking leads to abstinence of alcohol and every other addiction. And, **an encounter with Christ is most sobering**. For instance, just look at how Peter responded in his first encounter with Christ!

When Simon Peter saw it, he fell down at Jesus' knees, saying, Depart from me; for I am a sinful man, O Lord.
Luke 5:8

And of course, there are many, many more examples.
It would make an interesting study!

One of the most remarkable things about the Christian life is that we can reach sobriety at its highest level, at any given moment, through the connection that we have with Our God who became one of us!

Fear

And there were in the same country shepherds abiding in the field, keeping watch over their flock by night. And, lo, the angel of the Lord came upon them, and the glory of the Lord shone round about them: and they were sore afraid. And the angel said unto them, Fear not: for, behold, I bring you good tidings of great joy, which shall be to all people. For unto you is born this day in the city of David a Saviour, which is Christ the Lord.
Luke 2:8-11

Although I have not engaged in every addiction that there is, I can boldly say that every addiction cultivates fear. The main reason that I am certain of this is because addictions are not of God.

During the first advent of Christ the angel says, "fear not". Many year later Jesus said to Him disciples, "*Peace I leave with you, my peace I give unto you: not as the world giveth, give I unto you. Let not your heart be troubled, neither let it be afraid*" (John 14:27). He is saying the same to us today as we choose Him over addictions and whatever else the world would offer.

Total Transformation

He shall be great, and shall be called the Son of the Highest.
Luke 1:32a

I love the expression of just what took place when Jesus was born; "The Son of God became the Son of man, so that the sons of men could become the sons of God". But, this expression will not be fully recognized so long as addictions deface the image which we were all born to bear. Thank God that there will come a day when everything that destroys that image will be done away with. That day came for my dad on December 14, 2014.

As dad faithfully maintained an intimate relationship with Jesus, despite dealing with the sufferings of muscular dystrophy, he took joy in the 'partial' transformation that is in Christ and looked forward to a complete transformation. He looked forward to the day that his ability to walk would be restored (he could not walk the last 20 years of his life). And, he, also, looked forward to the day that he would no longer sin. His favorite bible verses reflect how he longed for this complete transformation.

Behold, what manner of love the Father hath bestowed upon us, that we should be called the sons of God: therefore the world knoweth us not, because it knew him not. Beloved, now are we the sons of God, and it doth not yet appear what we shall be: but we know that, when he shall appear, we shall be like him; for we shall see him as he is. 1 John 3:1-2 KJV

You are the Gift

And when they were come into the house, they saw the young child with Mary his mother, and fell down, and worshipped him: and when they had opened their treasures, they presented unto him gifts; gold, and frankincense and myrrh.
Mathew 2:11

Remember the story of the 'little drummer boy' who was present during this occasion? It is said that while the wise men gave their expensive gifts to the new born King, all the little drummer boy had to offer was a drum performance. While the intention of the story writer may have been good, I would have to differ over whether a drum performance was all that the little drummer boy had to give. You might say that the performance is included in what the little drummer boy had to offer. **He had himself to offer. We all do.**

2 Corinthians 8:5 is an example of this.

And this they did, not as we hoped, but first gave their own selves to the Lord, and unto us by the will of God.

If there is one thing that I can say about addictions is that we give ourselves to them body and soul (belongings as well). This is why addictions can be accurately defined as idols. Whatever it is that we worship, we make sacrifices for, we allow it to dominate us, and we give it glory and honor.

I like the illustration given by Chuck Swindoll in his book "Improving Your Serve: The Art of Unselfish Living" describing the relationship that God is calling us to.

"I want this pearl. How much is it?" "Well," the seller says, "it's very expensive." "But, how much?" we ask. "Well, a very large amount." "Do you think I could buy it?" "Oh, of course, everyone can buy it." "But, didn't you say it was very expensive?" "Yes." "Well, how much is it?" "Everything you have," says the seller. We make up our minds, "All right, I'll buy it," we say. "Well, what do you have?" he wants to know. "Let's write it down." "Well, I have ten thousand dollars in the bank." "Good- -ten thousand dollars. What else?" "That's all. That's all I have." "Well, I have a few dollars here in my pocket." "How much?" We start digging. "Well, let's see--thirty, forty, sixty, eighty, a hundred, a hundred twenty dollars." "That's fine. What else do you have?" "Well, nothing. That's all." "Where do you live?" He's still probing. "In my house. Yes, I have a house." "The house, too, then." He writes that down. "You mean I have to live in my camper?" "You have a camper? That, too. What else?" "I'll have to sleep in my car!" "You have a car?" "Two of them." "Both become mine, both cars. What else?" "Well, you already have my money, my house, my camper, my cars. What more do you want?" "Are you alone in this world?" "No, I have a wife and two children...." "Oh, yes, your wife and children, too. What else?" "I have nothing left! I am left alone now." Suddenly the seller exclaims, "Oh, I almost forgot! You yourself, too! Everything becomes mine--wife, children, house, money, cars--and you too." Then he goes on. "Now listen--I will allow you to use all these things for the time being. But don't forget that they are mine, just as you are. And whenever I need any of them you must give them up, because now I am the owner."

Isn't He worthy?

The fulfillment of Christ

And I will put enmity between you and the woman, and between your offspring and hers; he will crush your head, and you will strike his heel.
Genesis 3:15

Here is the very first time that the birth of Christ is foretold. It is announced by God Himself. If it were not for God making the initiative to deal with my addictions then I would not be clean and sober. And as quiet as it is kept, that initiative began way back in eternity, as the Lamb of God was slain from the foundation of the world (Rev. 13:8) and pronounced in Genesis 3:15. While I am bereaved over R.C. Sproul's passing just the other day (12/14/18), I will borrow a comment from his ministry regarding Genesis 3:15.

"From the earliest times, Genesis 3:15 has been called the proto-evangelism because it is the first note of God's redemptive intention following the fall in the garden of Eden. When Adam and Eve failed to obey the terms of the covenant of works (Gen. 3:6), God did not destroy them (which would have served justice), but instead revealed His covenant of grace to them by promising a Savior (Gen. 3:15), one who would restore the kingdom that had latterly been destroyed."

The fact of the matter is that man was created to rule the earth, but Adam and Eve forfeited their rule to Satan because of their rebellion against God. We do the same with our addictions. Yet and still, God has given us the chance to regain our rule through Christ.

God loves us just as we are, and that He loves us too much to let us stay the way that we are.

Obedience

When Joseph woke up, he did what the angel of the Lord had commanded him and took Mary home as his wife.
Matthew 1:24

The angel gave the word of God concerning Christ to Joseph and Joseph obeyed. There is no substitute for obedience. James 1:22 says, "*Do not merely listen to the word, and so deceive yourselves. Do what it says.*" Then, in verse 25 we are told, "*whoever looks intently into the perfect law that gives freedom, and continues in it—not forgetting what they have heard, but doing it—they will be blessed in what they do.*"

How blessed we are to have the word of God as a weapon against addictions! *For the word of God is alive and active. Sharper than any double-edged sword, it penetrates even to dividing soul and spirit, joints and marrow; it judges the thoughts and attitudes of the heart* (Hebrews 4:12).

I was recently intrigued by the idea of how we are communicating with God and others by what we do. I think that it is interesting the way that this is expressed in the King James Version of the Bible with the word "conversation". Here are just a few examples which are both negative and positive:

That ye put off concerning the former conversation the old man, which is corrupt according to the deceitful lusts.
Ephesians 4:22

Only let your conversation be as it becometh the gospel of Christ.
Philippians 1:27a

The fact of the matter is, when we do what God says with the right kind of attitude, it is a practice of worship (as we **are <u>telling</u> God that He is worthy of our obedience**). This is what others 'hear' as well. And when we don't do as He says, or do it with a bad attitude, we are telling Him, as well as others, that He is not worthy. The love we express for God can be simplified into three basics.

1. Talking to God.
2. Listening to God.
3. Doing what God says.

Excitement

And it came to pass, as the angels were gone away from them into heaven, the shepherds said one to another, Let us now go even unto Bethlehem, and see this thing which is come to pass, which the Lord hath made known unto us.
Luke 2:15

It is amazing how God made known to the shepherds the birth of Christ. Prior to Jesus' arrival, Israel had not heard from God for hundreds of years. Ironically, the last word that God gave to Israel, before the arrival of Christ, was "a curse" (Malachi 4:6).

The most important thing for us who have been fooled into thinking that addictions are worthy of our lives is a word from God.

The last time that I turned from my addictions (6 years ago), my biggest fear was that God would never ever speak to me again. I honestly thought that He would not!

What an exciting time this was for the shepherds to whom the blessing of Israel (and all mankind) was announced. Just yesterday, as the Lord brought an exciting chain of events, I was reminded of a prayer that I made to God when I decided to give Him my all.

I was, basically, being honest with God of how I had found so much excitement in my drug use and that I needed Him to change me or to provide just as much excitement (if not more), as I followed Him. I am tremendously grateful that God has honored that prayer! As He continues to reveal to me the magnificence of Christ, I can see why the shepherds were so excited upon the announcement of His birth!

Casualties

Then Herod, when he saw that he was mocked of the wise men, was exceeding wroth, and sent forth, and slew all the children that were in Bethlehem, and in all the coasts thereof, from two years old and under, according to the time which he had diligently inquired of the wise men.
Matthew 2:16

What we see here is the rejection of Christ before He even spoke a word. This is expressed many times in scripture. And this is the very worst habit there is. In fact, I believe, that the habit of rejecting

Christ is ultimately where all other bad habits originate.

It was because Herod did not want to relinquish his rule to this newborn King, that slew all the children, hoping that he would kill Jesus also.
Addictions do not want Jesus to rule either. I mourn over how addictions kill, misuse, and abuse children as well. Some say that many addictions are 'victimless'. I would beg to differ, when you look at all the children that are harmed and/or neglected because of addictions. I long for the day when Christ will take His rightful place. May we do all that we can to make this a reality in our own lives until that day!

Seeking the Lord

Now when Jesus was born in Bethlehem of Judaea in the days of Herod the king, behold, there came wise men from the east to Jerusalem, Saying, Where is he that is born King of the Jews? for we have seen his star in the east, and are come to worship him.
Matthew 2:1-2

Wise men pursue and anticipate Wisdom (personified, just as Christ is called the wisdom of God, 1 Cor. 1:24). Most worthy! My wife and I were reminiscing yesterday of how we would anticipate Christmas day, as children still do. I

thought of how it was almost like an addiction. Then, I thought of how intense my pursuit and anticipation were for the addictions that I once indulged in. I love the way that the scriptures lead us into doing just the opposite of what our flesh would have us do. Forgive me for not giving references (I will just name a few phrases).
Turned to God from idols
Put off the old man, put on the new
Let him who stole steal no more...let him give

Need I say that the pursuit and anticipation of an addiction is foolish? Not only is it ungodly, it is unrewarding. As it has been said for many years- "Wise men still seek Him" (Christ)!

Stillness vs. Alienation

And Mary said, My soul doth magnify the Lord. And my spirit hath rejoiced in God my Saviour. For he hath regarded the low estate of his handmaiden: for, behold, from henceforth all generations shall call me blessed. For he that is mighty hath done to me great things; and holy is his name.
Luke 1:46-49 (KJV)

There's a certain stillness in this passage. It comes from Mary following the will of God. Stillness is something that cannot be found in addictions.

Within that stillness, Mary knows that she is safe (in the arms of God). Again, something that cannot be found in addictions. There is a union with God for Mary. Addictions are caused by alienation from God leading to further estrangement from Him. Just look at Edward T. Welch's definition of addictions and compare it with Mary's experience with God!

Arising out of our alienation from the Living God, addiction is bondage to the rule of a substance, activity, or state of mind, which then becomes the center of life, defending itself from the truth, and leading to further estrangement from God's kingdom.

"Addictions: A Banquet in the Grave" and "Running in Circles"

Your Own Understanding

And without controversy great is the mystery of godliness: God was manifest in the flesh, justified in the Spirit, seen of angels, preached unto the Gentiles, believed on in the world, received up into glory.
1 Timothy 3:16 (KJV)

I would be the first to admit that there are many things that I don't understand. I often tell people that if I could explain to you exactly how God became a man, then I would be God. There are some things that we will never ever be capable of understanding (even with a glorified mind and body).

The most difficult thing of dealing with an addiction is that we strive to understand our heart (which is impossible outside of God's help). Just as Jesus told Peter that flesh and blood had not revealed the true nature of Christ to him (Matt.16:17), we need the Father to show us our heart. Jeremiah 17:9 says, "*the heart is deceitful above all things, and it is exceedingly perverse and corrupt and severely, mortally sick! Who can know [perceive, understand, be acquainted with] his own heart and mind?*" (Amplified Version).

Verse 10 says, "*I, the Lord, search and examine the mind, I test the heart, To give to each man according to his ways, According to the results of his deeds.*"

Great is our Lord, and of great power: his understanding is infinite (Psalms 147:5).

The Mind of Christ

Let this mind be in you, which was also in Christ Jesus: Who, being in the form of God, thought it not robbery to be equal with God: But made himself of no reputation, and took upon him the form of a

servant, and was made in the likeness of men: And being found in fashion as a man, he humbled himself, and became obedient unto death, even the death of the cross.
Philippians 2:5-8 (KJV)
Where is your head? What kind of mind do you have? This is what determines how you respond to the things that the world offers and whether you will succumb to an addiction.

Years ago, in a class, I was most impressed with the statement that Jesus was more human than anyone who had ever lived. Addictions are not human. In many cases, addictions exhibit cruel, barbaric, savage, selfish behavior.

It is no wonder that God has told us in Psalms 32:8 to not be as the horse or the mule.

Through Jesus we can be human as well. We are born again once we confess that we are not the people that God intended us to be (right from birth) and ask Jesus to save us. We rely on the blood of Christ for the forgiveness of our sins. And then, we make the choice to deny ourselves and rely on the power of Christ to change us into who God wants us to be each day. It is no wonder why Jesus said to take his yoke upon us and learn of Him.

Sobriety, abstinence, sanctification, transformation, recovery (whatever word that you want to use) is

fueled by humility. Pastor Rick Warren says, "True humility is not thinking less of yourself; it is thinking of yourself less."
Think upon Jesus!

Deceived by Satan

And she brought forth her firstborn son, and wrapped him in swaddling clothes, and laid him in a manger; because there was no room for them in the inn. And there were in the same country shepherds abiding in the field, keeping watch over their flock by night. And, lo, the angel of the Lord came upon them, and the glory of the Lord shone round about them: and they were sore afraid.
Luke 2:7-9 (KJV)

Some would argue whether the birth of Christ was the most glorious moment in history, or whether the day that He paid for our sins on the cross was the most glorious. One thing that we all can pretty much agree on is **that there is no glory in an addiction**. Unfortunately, the devil wants us to believe that there is. I still remember my very first encounter with crack cocaine, and how I felt that it was what I had been looking for all my life. I did not realize how deeply I had been deceived by Satan and my own flesh. We are warned of this in Isaiah 5:20.

Woe unto them that call evil good, and good evil; that put darkness for light, and light for darkness; that put bitter for sweet, and sweet for bitter!

Praise God for the light that is in Christ! John said that Jesus was the true light (John 1:9). Praise God for showing us that light! Jesus Himself said, "*many prophets and righteous men have desired to see those things which ye see, and have not seen them; and to hear those things which ye hear, and have not heard them.*"

Therefore we ought to give the more earnest heed to the things which we have heard, lest at any time we should let them slip.
Hebrews 2:1 (KJV)

Sharing

And when they had seen it, they made known abroad the saying which was told them concerning this child.
Luke 2:17 (KJV)

Sharing is essential to life. As addictions live on because we share just what they can do, how 'magnificent' they are, so they are conquered as we tell others of the wonders of Christ. Sharing Christ is essential to the lives of those who think that life is found in whatever it is that the world has to offer. I have an ongoing saying whenever someone looks at a commercial and says, "That looks good". I respond by saying, "It's supposed to. No one is going to advise something by telling you how bad it is." Whether the 'product' is good or not, they will tell you that it is good for *their own* benefit (so that you will give them your money).

Satan wants you to think that his products are the best thing ever. The bottom line is that whether people place their faith in an addiction or their faith in Christ, someone has shared with them the' life' that is found in either. Ironically, the life of an addiction is death. For the wages of sin is death, but the gift of God is eternal life through Jesus Christ our Lord (Rom. 6:23). The most tremendous gift of all!

The Joy of Christmas

The joy of Christmas is our sobriety/sanity. Many years ago, while attending an Alcoholics Anonymous meeting, I listened to a speaker who had such broken English that I thought that I heard him say that he was 'merciful' during the many times that he had stopped drinking and so he would go back to drinking time and time again. Over and over, the speaker said that he was "very merciful" when he stopped drinking. Towards the end of his speech, I finally realized that the speaker had been telling us that he had been "miserable" during those times of abstinence (without true fellowship with God). While God wants us to be merciful in our walk with Him, He does not want us to be miserable. George Muller said that, "the first great and primary business to which I ought to attend every day is have my soul happy in the Lord". Muller is credited for saying that, "our first duty as Christians is to get ourselves happy in God". Nehemiah 8:10 says that **the joy of the Lord is your strength**.

References

Lewis, C.S., *Mere Christianity* (HarperOne, 2015)

Lockyer, Herbert, *All the Divine Names and Titles in the Bible* (Zondervan, 1975)

Ortiz, Juan Carlos, *Disciple* (Wheaton, IL: Creation House, 1975)

Thomas, Derek, *The Significance of Genesis 3:15* (Ligonier Ministries, 2018)

Unger, Merrill, F, *The New Unger's Bible Dictionary* (Moody Press, 2007)

Warren, Rick, quotation

Welch, Edward T., *Addictions: A Banquet in the Grave* (P&R Publishing, 2001)

Westminster Shorter Catechism (number 1)

Sobriety for Christmas was adopted from the writing of Gregory Madison's ***Bible Verses Addictions*** and bears the philosophy concerning addictions that is found is his book ***Turning to God from Idols: A Biblical Approach to Additions.***

For further readings please visit one or all the following:
www.turningtogodfromidols.com
www.facebook.com/sobrietyinChrist/
www.facebook.com/turningtoGodfromidols/
www.facebook.com/aweinawe/

Made in the USA
Monee, IL
05 November 2026

67352877R00025